Metamorphic Rocks

by Melissa Stewart

Heinemann Library
CHICAGO, ILLINOIS

Designed by Ox and Company

An Editorial Directions book

Printed in Hong Kong

06 05 04 03 02
10 9 8 7 6 5 4 3 2 1

Library of Congress Cataloging-in-Publication Data
Stewart, Melissa.
  Metamorphic rocks / Melissa Stewart.
    p. cm.—(Rocks and minerals)
Includes bibliographical references and index.
Summary: Provides an overview of metamorphic rocks including how they were formed,
where they are found, their characteristics, history, significance, and uses.
  ISBN: 1-58810-257-2 (HC), 1-4034-0093-8 (Pbk.)
  1. Rocks, Metamorphic—Juvenile literature. [1. Rocks, Metamorphic. 2. Geology.] I. Title.
  QE475.A2 S78 2002
  552'.4—dc21   2001002758

Acknowledgments
The author and publishers are grateful to the following for permission to reproduce copyright material:

Photographs ©: Cover background, H.H. Thomas/Unicorn Stock Photos; cover foreground, Martin Miller/Visuals Unlimited,
Inc.; p. 4, Cameramann International, Ltd.; p. 5, Grace Davies Photography; p. 7, John Springer/Bettmann/Corbis; p. 10 top,
Tom Bean; p. 10 bottom, Gerald & Buff Corsi/Visuals Unlimited, Inc.; p. 11, M. Long/Visuals Unlimited, Inc.; p. 12, Sylvester
Allred/Visuals Unlimited, Inc.; p.13, A.J. Copley/Visuals Unlimited, Inc.; p. 14, Keystone/The Image Works; p. 15, Joseph L.
Fontenot/Visuals Unlimited, Inc.; p. 17, Corbis; p. 18, Tom Bean; p. 19, Roger Ressmeyer/Corbis; p. 20, Maurice Nimmo/Frank
Lane Photo Agency/Corbis; p. 21, Townsend P. Dickinson/The Image Works; p. 22, Grace Davies Photography; p. 23, Adam
Tanner/The Image Works; p. 24 top, Doug Sokell/Visuals Unlimited, Inc.; p. 24 bottom, Gary Milburn/Tom Stack &
Associates; p. 26, Glenn Oliver/Visuals Unlimited, Inc.; p. 27, B. Daemmrich/The Image Works; p. 28, Grace Davies
Photography; p. 29, Mark E. Gibson/Visuals Unlimited, Inc.

Some words are shown in bold, **like this.** You can find out what they mean by looking in the glossary.

Contents

What Is a Rock?.................... 4

Layers of Earth.................. 6

Land on the Move................ 8

Three Kinds of Rocks 10

How Metamorphic Rock Forms 12

A Look at Mountains................ 14

Too Hot to Touch 16

A Shocking Experience................ 18

How People Use Metamorphic Rock 20

Magnificent Marble................ 22

The Rock Cycle................ 24

Is That a Metamorphic Rock?........... 26

Be a Rock Hound................ 28

Glossary................................ 30

To Find Out More 31

Index........................... 32

What Is a Rock?

Rocks come in all shapes and sizes. Small rocks are often called "pebbles." Some people call medium-sized rocks "stones." A rock that is too large to pick up and carry around is a "boulder." You see rocks every day, but do you ever stop to take a closer look? You can tell a lot about a rock by examining it for just a few minutes. Is it smooth or rough? Is it shiny or dull?

Taroko Gorge divides some of Taiwan's most impressive metamorphic rocks. The gorge was formed as the Limu River cut through 12 miles (19 kilometers) of marble and granite.

The next time you go for a ride in the car, look for places where workers have blasted through rock to build the road. Notice the rock's colors and patterns. Do you see layers that seem twisted or folded? If so, you are probably looking at metamorphic rock. Many mountains are made of metamorphic rock.

DID YOU KNOW?

Eclogite is a metamorphic rock. Some people call it Christmas tree rock because it is green with small, round pieces of a red mineral called garnet.

Metamorphic rock is one of three kinds of rocks found in the world. The other two kinds are **sedimentary rock** and **igneous rock.** We will learn more about how metamorphic rock forms later in this book. Each kind of rock forms in a different way, but they are all made of **minerals.**

A mineral is a natural solid material. No matter where you find it, a mineral always has the same chemical makeup and the same structure. In other words, the **atoms** that mix together to form a specific mineral always arrange themselves in the same way. Most minerals have a **crystal** structure. Crystals usually have a regular shape and smooth, flat sides called faces.

Schist is one kind of metamorphic rock. It forms at high pressure and low temperature. Schist contains quartz, feldspar, mica, and other minerals.

Schist is a metamorphic rock that usually contains minerals of biotite, mica, feldspar, and quartz. The crystal structure of quartz is made up of silicon and oxygen atoms that are always arranged in the same way. A quartz crystal always has six faces.

SCIENCE IN ACTION

Petrologists—scientists who study rocks—can identify a rock by knowing where it came from and by looking at the **properties** of its minerals. For example, petrologists examine the color, the shininess, and the hardness of the minerals in a rock. They also study the size, shape, and arrangement of the crystals.

Layers of Earth

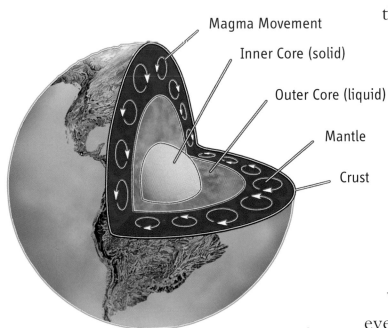

Magma Movement

Inner Core (solid)

Outer Core (liquid)

Mantle

Crust

The thin outer layer of Earth is the crust. The next layer, the mantle, is made of magma that is constantly moving. The core is made of an outer liquid core and an inner solid core.

To understand metamorphic rocks, we must know something about the structure of Earth. Most of our planet is made of rock. When you dig into the ground, you find soil. Soil is made of broken-up rock mixed with rotting plant and animal material. If you dig deeper, you will eventually hit solid rock. The soil and the layer of hard rock beneath it make up the **crust.**

Below the crust is a thick layer of molten **magma.** This hot, liquid rock forms Earth's **mantle.** The heat that keeps magma partially melted comes

DID YOU KNOW?

Earth's crust can be anywhere from 3 to 43 miles (5 to 69 kilometers) thick. The thickest parts are below tall mountains of metamorphic rock. The thinnest parts are underneath the oceans.

from Earth's **core.** The outer core is made of metals that have melted to form a gooey liquid. The inner core is made of solid metals. The weight of these overlying layers presses down on the inner core. All that pressure holds the **molecules** that make up the inner core so close together that they cannot turn into a liquid.

Heat energy from the core naturally tries to escape to a cooler place. As heat moves from the core into the mantle, it squeezes magma like toothpaste trapped inside a tube. As the hottest magma near the core is forced toward the crust, cooler magma moves down to take its place. Over millions of years, magma slowly circles through the mantle.

WHAT A TRIP!

Since ancient times, people have wondered what the inside of Earth is like. In 1864, a French writer named Jules Verne wrote a science-fiction novel called *Journey to the Center of the Earth*. In 1959, the book was made into a film (left). Both tell the story of four people who enter a **volcano** on Iceland and travel all the way to Earth's fiery core. Along the way, they see a cave filled with enormous mushrooms and dinosaur-like monsters that live far below Earth's surface. Of course, there aren't really mushrooms or giant reptiles deep underground.

Land on the Move

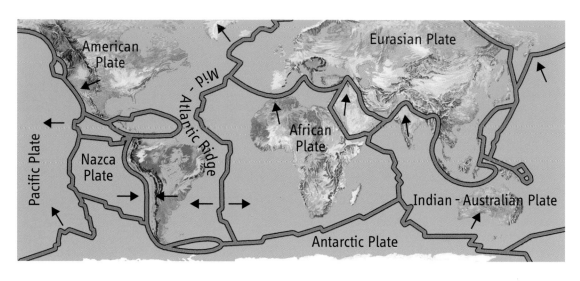

American Plate

Eurasian Plate

Mid - Atlantic Ridge

Pacific Plate

Nazca Plate

African Plate

Indian - Australian Plate

Antarctic Plate

Earth's surface is broken into many plates. The major plates are labeled on this diagram. The plates are moving constantly, though very slowly, in the direction of the arrows. The Mid-Atlantic Ridge is a rift formed by two plates moving apart.

Earth's **crust** has a lot in common with the crust on top of a chicken pot pie. The pie's crust rests on top of thick, steaming-hot gravy full of chicken chunks, peas, and carrots. Earth's crust rests on top of a sea of molten **magma.** Before you eat a chicken pot pie, you cut its crust into pieces. Earth's crust is broken into large pieces called **plates.**

As magma circles through the **mantle,** the plates that make up Earth's crust move too. In some parts of the world, plates move apart and long cracks called **rifts** are left behind. When rifts form under the ocean, the material from the mantle rises to the surface and creates new land on each side of the rift. This process is called **seafloor spreading.**

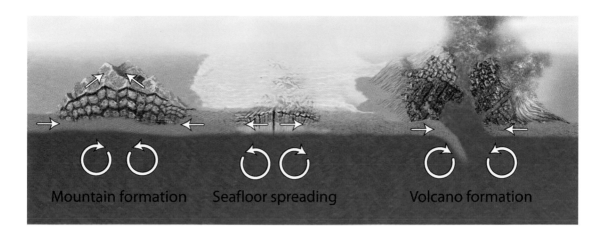

Mountain formation   Seafloor spreading   Volcano formation

When rifts form on land, earthquakes may shake the ground and **volcanoes** may erupt, spilling lava out over the land.

In other parts of the world, plates bump into one another. Sometimes one plate slides over the other. Then the bottom plate moves down into the mantle, where it melts. When two plates crash and push against each other with great force, the land buckles and tall mountains form. When two plates scrape against each other, the result is a **transform fault,** such as the San Andreas Fault in California and the Dalkey Fault in Ireland. When enough pressure builds up along a fault, an earthquake occurs.

Mountains may form when two plates hit head-on. The seafloor expands as magma rises through a rift. When one plate moves below another, magma may rise to the surface and escape through a volcano.

MOUNTAINS IN MOTION

Mount Everest, the tallest mountain in the world, is made of metamorphic rock. It is part of the Himalaya Mountains. The mountains in this range get a little taller every year as the Indian-Australian Plate crashes into the Eurasian Plate.

Three Kinds of Rocks

Limestone is one kind of sedimentary rock. It contains calcite, dolomite, aragonite, and other minerals.

As we have seen, Earth has three kinds of rocks—**sedimentary, igneous,** and metamorphic. Each kind of rock forms in a different way. Igneous rock forms when **magma** from Earth's **mantle** cools and hardens. Sometimes the magma forces its way to Earth's surface and spills onto the land as lava. Over time, large **volcanic** mountains of igneous rock pile up. This kind of igneous rock cools quickly and has very small **crystals.** In other cases, pools of magma become trapped at the top of the mantle and cool slowly over thousands of years. Some of the largest and most beautiful crystals in the world were formed in this way. Granite, gabbro, basalt, and obsidian are examples of igneous rock.

Obsidian is a dark, volcanic glass. It forms when lava cools very quickly.

Sedimentary rock forms as layers of mud, clay, sand, and other materials build up over time. The weight of the materials at the top of the pile presses down on the materials below. All that pressure cements the materials together to form hard rock. If you look closely at sedimentary rock, you may be able to see its layers. Limestone, sandstone, shale, and conglomerate are examples of sedimentary rock.

Metamorphic rock forms when heat or pressure changes the **minerals** within igneous rock, sedimentary rock, or another metamorphic rock. This often happens when Earth's **plates** collide. Marble, slate, gneiss, hornfels, phyllite, migmatite, serpentinite, quartzite, and schist are examples of metamorphic rock.

Marble is a metamorphic rock that forms when limestone is placed under stress. If the limestone was pure, the marble will be white. If the limestone contained impurities, the marble may be black, green, red, or yellowish brown.

IMAGINE THAT!

Would you like a dog or cat, but your parents say, "No way"? In the 1970s, kids who wanted an easy-to-care-for companion found a new idea—the pet rock. For a few years, pet rocks were sold in stores across the United States. Whether they were igneous, sedimentary, or metamorphic, these unusual "pets" had many advantages. They didn't need to be fed or walked. They were also small enough to fit in a person's pocket, and they were very well behaved.

How Metamorphic Rock Forms

You can clearly see the folds in the metamorphic rock that makes up the Canadian Rockies. The Rocky Mountains formed about 65 million years ago.

DID YOU KNOW?

As **sedimentary** and igneous rocks transform into metamorphic rock, **atoms** from one mineral sometimes sneak into a different mineral's crystal structure. When this happens, beautiful new crystals of sapphire, ruby, peridot, garnet, emerald, and other prized **gemstones** may form.

The extreme conditions that create metamorphic rocks cause the **minerals** in the rock to change into different minerals. Some metamorphic rock is made when rock is heated, folded, and squeezed during mountain building. This process is clearly shown in the exposed layers of rock that form the peaks of the Canadian Rocky Mountains in British Columbia. (To learn more about more metamorphic rock and mountains, see pages 14–15.)

Other metamorphic rock forms when rocks are heated by streams of **magma** that spurt up into the crust. The sizzling-hot magma bakes the surrounding rock, turning it into metamorphic rock. Meanwhile, the magma itself eventually cools and forms **igneous rock.** Examples of this

HOW HEAT AND PRESSURE CHANGE ROCK

ORIGINAL ROCK	NEW METAMORPHIC ROCK
Basalt (igneous)	Serpentinite
Granite (igneous)	Gneiss
Limestone (sedimentary)	Marble
Phyllite (metamorphic)	Schist
Sandstone (sedimentary)	Quartzite
Schist (metamorphic)	Gneiss
Shale (sedimentary)	Slate
Slate (metamorphic)	Phyllite

process are more common below Earth's surface. For this type of metamorphic rock to be seen, all the material above and around the area must be **eroded** over millions of years.

Because the minerals that make up metamorphic rock have had to endure tremendous heat and pressure, the resulting rock is hard and tough. Gneiss is especially durable because it forms when other kinds of metamorphic rock are altered. This rock usually has large, interlocking **crystals.** The color of a gneiss specimen depends on the minerals it contains.

Gneiss is one of the toughest kinds of rock in the world. Because it forms deep underground, it can be seen only in uplifted mountain ranges or in areas that have been severely eroded.

A Look at Mountains

Nearly all the world's major mountain ranges are made up mostly of metamorphic rock. The Himalayas in Asia, the Alps and Caledonian Mountains in Europe, and the Appalachian Mountains and Rocky Mountains in North America all contain metamorphic rock.

The Alps in France and Switzerland are made of metamorphic rock. They formed more than two million years ago as the African Plate collided with the Eurasian Plate.

Mountains often form when Earth's **plates** collide. Over long periods of time, the pressure of the bumping plates pushes land areas together and lifts them up. As the rock is twisted and squeezed, huge folded mountains of metamorphic rock rise into the air.

DID YOU KNOW?

Tall mountain ranges sometimes affect weather by blocking cloud movements. As a result, it is often very wet on one side of a mountain range and very dry on the other side. Think about this as you look at the locations of Earth's deserts.

14

Not all mountains are made of metamorphic rock. Block mountains form when plate movements break large areas of land into many giant pieces. Some of these pieces, or blocks, are forced up and form mountains. Other blocks are forced down to form valleys. This is what happened in the part of the American West called the Great Basin.

Some mountains are made of lava—**magma** that spills onto Earth's surface through a **volcano.** As the lava cools, it hardens and forms mountain-sized piles. Some of the most spectacular volcanic mountains in the world include Mount Kilimanjaro in Tanzania, Africa, and Mauna Loa in Hawaii.

A CLUE TO THE PAST

Scientists have discovered that the Appalachian Mountains (above) in the United States are part of the same ancient mountain range as the Caledonian Mountains that run through Great Britain and Norway. How is this possible?

Millions of years ago, North America and Europe were part of the same huge continent. Today, the American Plate is moving away from the Eurasian Plate, and the Atlantic Ocean is getting a little wider every year.

Too Hot to Touch

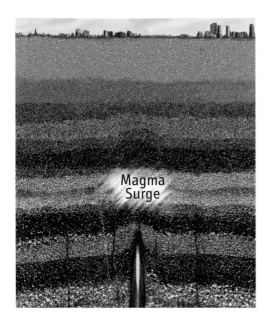

Magma
Surge

When Earth's **plates** slam together, the force affects large areas of rock. That is why metamorphic mountain chains are often thousands of miles long. Smaller areas of metamorphic rock form in a different way. Sometimes molten **magma** escapes from Earth's **mantle** and creeps into the **crust.** These **magma surges** can be as small as a room in your house.

In some parts of the world, magma surges spike through the crust. The rock that comes into contact with the hot magma is transformed into metamorphic rock.

Sometimes the magma blasts all the way to Earth's surface and spills onto the land through **volcanoes.** In many cases, however, the magma is not able to travel all the way through the crust. The trapped magma surge really heats up the surrounding rock. As a result, the **minerals** in the rock that touches the magma can change quite a bit. Farther away from the surge site, the scorching magma has less effect.

As the magma surge cools, it forms a column of **igneous rock.** At the same time, nearby rock is

DID YOU KNOW?

Hornfels is a metamorphic rock that forms when shale, a sedimentary rock, comes into contact with a magma surge. As the magma superheats the rock, the minerals that make up shale rearrange themselves and form the **crystal** structure of hornfels.

transformed into metamorphic rock. Split Mountain in California is a perfect example of this process. When you look at some parts of this formation, you can see a dark layer of metamorphic rock on top of a lighter layer of igneous rock. The igneous rock was once a magma surge. It heated the **sedimentary rock** above and turned it into metamorphic rock. Later, the entire area was lifted up and became part of Earth's surface.

Split Mountain in California has distinct layers of metamorphic and igneous rock. This is clear evidence that a magma surge once existed in this area.

A Shocking Experience

Most metamorphic rock forms slowly over millions of years. The tremendous heat and pressure inside Earth needs time to affect **minerals** in ways that transform them into metamorphic rock. But there is a way to make metamorphic rock at lightning speed.

When a bolt of lightning strikes sand, the grains may fuse together and form a solid metamorphic rock called fulgurite. Scientists call this process shock metamorphism. Fulgurite is very fragile, so it is unusual to find long pieces of this rock. The world's longest fulgurite sample was found by researchers at the University of Florida in 1996. The shocked strip is 17 feet (5.2 meters) long.

Shock metamorphism can also happen when a **meteorite** strikes Earth's surface. As a space rock falls through Earth's **atmosphere,** particles in the air rub against it and create a force called **friction.** Friction generates a lot of heat. When the object crashes into the ground, it can transfer all its heat energy to whatever it hits. As the force and energy strike our planet's surface, minerals in

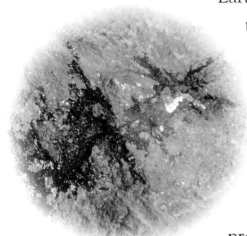

A smooth, glassy line of fulgurite runs through this rock. This tells scientists that lightning once struck the rock.

the rocky layers close to the surface can instantly rearrange themselves to form metamorphic rock. Meteorite craters lined with metamorphic rock have been discovered in many parts of the world, including Australia and Mexico. Giant meteorite craters can also be seen on the surface of Mercury, Mars, and many of the moons in our solar system.

WHAT A DISCOVERY!

In the 1950s, Eugene Shoemaker began to study Meteor Crater near Flagstaff, Arizona. Shoemaker was a geologist— a scientist who studies rocks to try to understand how Earth formed and how it has changed over time. By studying the crater, Shoemaker discovered that the area was once made of **sedimentary rock.** About 25,000 years ago, a tremendous force had suddenly transformed rock at the surface of the crater into metamorphic rock. This proved that a meteorite had created Meteor Crater. Although Meteor Crater is about 4,000 feet (1,220 meters) across, the space rock that created the giant hole was only about 100 feet (30 meters) wide.

How People Use Metamorphic Rock

Rock is one of Earth's most valuable **natural resources.** Some kinds of rock contain deposits of oil and natural gas. Important **minerals,** metals, and precious **gemstones** are found in rock, too.

Rhodochrosite is a mineral commonly found in metamorphic rock. It contains the metal manganese, which is added to iron during the steel-making process.

The metamorphic rock schist is mined because it sometimes contains large garnet **crystals.** Garnet is usually blood-red, but it may also be yellow, light green, or colorless. This gem has been prized for centuries and is frequently used to make jewelry.

The minerals chromite and rhodochrosite are often found in metamorphic rock. Chromite contains the metal chromium—an important ingredient in stainless steel. Chromium makes stainless steel hard and prevents it from rusting. Rhodochrosite is used to make batteries and to purify drinking water.

Talc and graphite are minerals that form only in metamorphic rock. Because talc is readily available, soft, and heat resistant, it is used to make baby powder, paper, paints, soap, fireproof roofing, linoleum, electrical insulation, and pottery. Graphite, another soft mineral, is used as the "lead" in pencils.

Serpentinite is a metamorphic rock that looks similar to green marble, and the two rocks are often confused. But serpentinite and marble contain different minerals. Serpentinite is made of the mineral serpentine. Marble contains calcite or dolomite and small amounts of other minerals. Like marble, serpentinite is soft enough to carve and polish. Many artists create beautiful sculptures and jewelry from serpentinite.

Quartzite is a very hard rock made of tightly packed grains of sand. It is sometimes used to build roads. It is also the perfect material for millstones used to grind wheat into flour and corn into corn meal.

Slate splits easily into flat pieces. It is sometimes used to make roofing tiles, like those seen here.

Magnificent Marble

By far the most widely used metamorphic rock is marble. This important metamorphic rock forms when layers of limestone are exposed to tremendous heat and pressure. Large regions of natural marble can be seen in the Alps and at the Oregon Caves National Monument.

Marble is beautiful and comes in many colors, including pure white, black, green, red, and yellowish brown. It is also easy to cut and polish. The Washington Monument and the Lincoln Memorial in Washington, D.C., are both made of marble. So are parts of the Parthenon in Greece.

The Taj Mahal houses the tombs of Mumtaz Mahal and her husband, Shah Jahan. The main building took eleven years to build, and the smaller buildings and gardens took another ten years to complete.

DID YOU KNOW?

Most of the world's caves are carved out of **sedimentary rock,** such as limestone. Oregon Caves National Monument is one of the few sites where water has slowly dissolved tough metamorphic rock to create long, winding passageways full of beautiful rocky formations.

EASY DOES IT

Most of the rock used to construct buildings and roads is removed from quarries in large slabs. To loosen the rock and break it into manageable pieces, workers at most quarries blast the area with dynamite. But marble is very delicate. The force of an explosion would cause marble to shatter. As a result, quarry workers must break up and remove marble by hand.

In the early 1600s, Mumtaz Mahal, the beautiful young wife of Indian emperor Shah Jahan, died unexpectedly. The emperor decided to build a stunning structure in memory of his beloved wife. The Taj Mahal is made of huge slabs of pure white marble that came from a quarry located more than 300 miles (483 kilometers) away from the building site in Agra, India. The heavy rock had to be transported in special carts pulled by oxen and elephants.

Marble is still being removed from this quarry near Carrara, Italy. The rock was created as the Apennine Mountains were lifted up millions of years ago.

People also use marble to make furniture, staircases, floor tiles, kitchen and bathroom countertops, and more. It can even be carved with a hammer and chisel to create beautiful sculptures. The famous Italian painter, sculptor, and architect Michelangelo (1475–1564) carved many incredible marble sculptures. All the rock Michelangelo used came from the Carrara quarry in Tuscany, Italy.

The Rock Cycle

Rocks are always changing. As Earth's **plates** ram into one another, rock deep below the surface is compressed and folded, lifting the land to create mighty mountains. In the process, metamorphic rock forms.

Weathering caused the fracture in this boulder. Heat and cold cause rocks to expand and contract, creating cracks that are deepened by water and ice.

While forces within Earth cause some metamorphic rock to rise above the surface, other metamorphic rock is exposed when water, wind, or glaciers **erode** the overlying rock. Rocks can also be broken down by plant roots, chemicals produced by tiny creatures that live in the soil, and repeated freezing and thawing. This is called **weathering.** Have you ever seen a boulder that looked as though it had mysteriously split in half? The split was probably the result of weathering.

DID YOU KNOW?

Metamorphic rock is very hard. It erodes and weathers more slowly than other kinds of rock. Nevertheless, marble sculptures around the world are threatened by **acid rain.** The chemicals in the rain slowly wear away the marble.

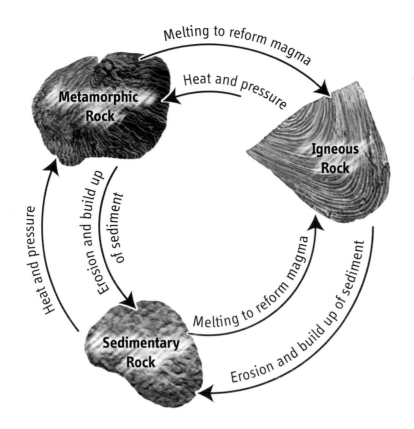

Melting to reform magma

Heat and pressure

Metamorphic Rock

Igneous Rock

Heat and pressure

Erosion and build up of sediment

Melting to reform magma

Erosion and build up of sediment

Sedimentary Rock

The rock we see on Earth today has not always been here. Rock forms and breaks down in a never-ending cycle.

As rock breaks down and wears away, the pieces are picked up by rivers and streams. Eventually, these **sediments** travel all the way to the ocean. Over time, layers of sediment build up and form **sedimentary rock.**

As Earth's plates move, some of the sedimentary rock is pulled into the **mantle,** where it melts and becomes **magma.** Eventually, some of that magma will cool to form **igneous rock.** Other areas of the sedimentary rock will be pressed and twisted. Under this tremendous pressure, they will form more metamorphic rock.

MOUNTAINS DON'T LAST FOREVER

The Rockies, the Andes, and the Himalayas all began to form between 60 and 70 million years ago. This makes them fairly young. Their peaks are still high, and their ridges are still sharp. The Appalachians and Urals are much older. They formed about 250 million years ago. Over time, much of the material that once made up these mountains has been worn away by wind and water. Some older mountains have eroded completely.

Is That a Metamorphic Rock?

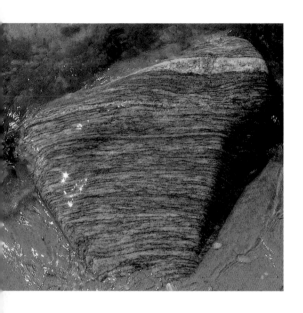

The banding in this gneiss sample makes it easy to identify it as a metamorphic rock. Have you ever seen rock with similar light and dark layers as you drove along a highway?

DID YOU KNOW?

Scientists have found quartzite in western Australia that is 3.5 billion years old. It may be the oldest metamorphic rock on Earth's surface.

Now that you've learned all about metamorphic rocks, you might want to search for some. How can you tell a metamorphic rock from other kinds of rocks? You can look for some telltale signs.

First, think about how metamorphic rock forms. Tremendous heat and pressure cause the **minerals** in other kinds of rock to be compressed, twisted, and rearranged. As a result, the minerals in metamorphic rock often face in the same direction and form light and dark bands. These characteristics are especially easy to see in samples of schist and gneiss. Sometimes the bands in metamorphic rock look stretched out and are easy to break into sheets. That's why people make roofs and walkways out of slate tiles.

Knowing where a rock comes from can also help you identify it. For example, if you find a rock near an ancient mountain chain, it may be a metamorphic rock. Metamorphic mountains often formed in places where large landmasses collided as Earth's **plates** moved.

To find out even more about a rock, you can study its **crystals.** Their color, shininess, and hardness can help you identify the minerals in the rock. Petrologists also pay close attention to the size, shape, and arrangement of the crystals in a rock. The crystals that make up metamorphic rock are usually small.

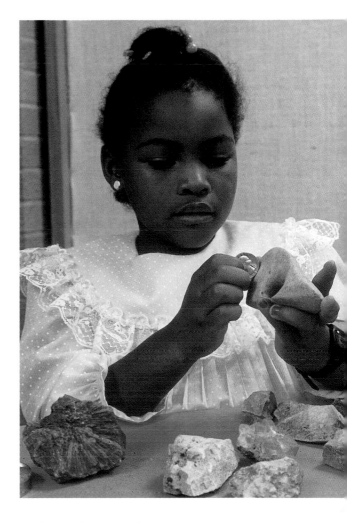

Of course, one of the best ways to identify a rock is to study a field guide to rocks and minerals. These books show pictures of rocks and give detailed descriptions of them.

You can identify rocks using the same techniques as scientists. Begin by studying the characteristics of the minerals that make up the sample.

CLUES FROM THE PAST

Fossils are most common in **sedimentary rock,** but they also occur in metamorphic rock that formed from sedimentary rock. The fossils in metamorphic rock often show signs of what the rock has endured. The ancient remains may be crushed, broken, squeezed, or stretched out.

Be a Rock Hound

The exterior of this building is made of gneiss. The banding pattern gives you a clue that this is a metamorphic rock.

Now that you know how to spot metamorphic rocks, you can begin searching for them. Look for marble in buildings and slate in walkways. You might also want to plan a rock hunting trip. There is plenty to see in the woods, in a field, or maybe even in your own backyard. Before you head out to an unfamiliar place, you will need to gather a few pieces of equipment and learn a few rules.

Once you have identified the rocks, it's a good idea to create a system for labeling, organizing, and storing them. Then you will always be able to find a specific sample later. You can arrange your specimens any way you like—by color, by **crystal** shape, by collection site, or even alphabetically. As your collection grows, being organized will become more and more important.

This impressive rock collection is housed at the University of Nevada at Reno. Each rock has been carefully labeled by a scientist.

WHAT YOU NEED

- Hiking boots
- A map and compass
- A pick and rock hammer to collect samples
- Safety glasses to keep rock chips out of your eyes
- A small paintbrush to remove dirt and extra rock chips from samples
- A camera to take photographs of rock formations
- A hand lens to get an up-close look at **minerals**
- A notebook for recording when and where you find each rock
- A field guide to rocks and minerals

WHAT YOU NEED TO KNOW

- Never go rock hunting alone. Go with a group that includes an adult.
- Know how to read a map and use a compass.
- Always get a landowner's permission before walking on private property. If you find interesting rocks, ask the owner if you may remove them.
- Before removing samples from public land, make sure rock collecting is allowed. Many natural rock formations are protected by law.
- Respect nature. Do not disturb living things, and do not litter.

Glossary

acid rain: rain that is polluted with acid in the atmosphere and that damages the environment

atmosphere: layer of air and other gases that surrounds Earth and some other planets

atom: smallest unit of an element that has all of the properties of the element

core: center of Earth. The inner core is solid, and the outer core is liquid.

crust: outer layer of Earth

crystal: repeating structural unit within most minerals

erode: to slowly wear away rock over time by the action of wind, water, or glaciers

fossil: remains or evidence of ancient life

friction: force that resists motion between two objects or surfaces. If there is motion and friction is created, energy is converted to heat.

gemstone: beautiful mineral that may be worn as jewelry

igneous rock: kind of rock that forms when magma from Earth's mantle cools and hardens

magma: hot, soft rock that makes up Earth's mantle. When magma spills out onto Earth's surface, it is called lava.

magma surge: magma that flows into cracks in Earth's crust and bakes the surrounding rock

mantle: layer of Earth between the crust and outer core. It is made of soft rock called magma.

meteorite: chunk of rock from space that hits Earth or another object in space

mineral: natural solid material with a specific chemical makeup and structure

molecule: smallest unit of a substance, made up of one or more atoms

natural resource: natural material that humans use to make important products

plate: one of the large slabs of rock that make up Earth's crust

property: trait or characteristic that helps make identification possible

rift: crack in Earth's surface created when two plates move away from each other

seafloor spreading: process that occurs when Earth's plates move apart, creating a crack on the floor of the ocean

sedimentary rock: kind of rock that forms as layers of mud, clay, and tiny rocks build up over time

sediment: mud, clay, or bits of rock picked up by rivers and streams and dumped in the ocean

transform fault: crack that forms on Earth's surface where two plates scrape against each other

volcano: crack in Earth's surface that extends into the mantle, and from which comes melted rock

weathering: breaking down of rock by plant roots or by repeated freezing and thawing

To Find Out More

BOOKS

Blobaum, Cindy. *Geology Rocks!: 50 Hands-On Activities to Explore the Earth*. Charlotte, Vt.: Williamson, 1999.

Christian, Peggy. *If You Find a Rock*. New York: Harcourt Brace, 2000.

Hiscock, Bruce. *The Big Rock*. New York: Aladdin, 1999.

Hopper, Merredith. *The Pebble in My Pocket: A History of Our Earth*. New York: Viking, 1994.

Kittinger, Jo S. *A Look at Rocks: From Coal to Kimberlite*. Danbury, Conn.: Franklin Watts, 1997.

Oldershaw, Cally. *3D-Eyewitness: Rocks and Minerals*. New York: Dorling Kindersley, 1999.

Pellant, Chris. *The Best Book of Fossils, Rocks, and Minerals*. New York: Kingfisher, 2000.

Ricciuti, Edward, and Margaret W. Carruthers. *National Audubon Society First Field Guide to Rocks and Minerals*. New York: Scholastic, 1998.

Staedter, Tracy. *Rocks and Minerals*. Pleasantville, N.Y.: Reader's Digest, 1999.

ORGANIZATIONS

Geological Survey of Canada
601 Booth Street
Ottawa, Ontario
KIA 0E8
613/995-3084

U.S. Geological Survey (USGS)
507 National Center
12201 Sunrise Valley Drive
Reston, VA 22092
703/648-4748

Index

Italicized page numbers indicate illustrations

acid rain 24
Alps 14, *14*, 22
American Plate *8*, 15
Andes Mountains 25
Apennine Mountains 23
Appalachian Mountains 15, *15*, 25
atoms 5, 12

basalt 10
biotite 5
block mountains 14

Caledonian Mountains 14, 15
Carrara quarry 23, *23*
chromite 20
collections 28–29, *29*
conglomerate 11
core 6, *6*, 7
crater 19, *19*
crust 6–7, *6*, 8, 16, *16*, 17
crystals 5, 10, 12, 13, 20, 27, 28

Dalkey Fault 9

earthquakes 9
eclogite 4
erosion 13, 24, 25
Eurasian Plate *8*, 9, 14, 15

faces 5
feldspar 5
field guides 27

formation 12–13, 18, 24
fossils 27
friction 18
fulgurite 18, *18*

gabbro 10
garnet 4, 20
gemstones 12, 20
geologists 19
gneiss 11, 13, *13*, 26, *26*, *28*
granite 4, 10, 20
graphite 21
Great Basin 15

Himalaya Mountains 9, 14, 25
hornfels 11, 16

identification 26–27, 28
igneous rock 4, 10, *10*, 12–13, 16–17, 20, 25, *25*
Indian-Australian Plate *8*, 9

Jahan, Shah 23
Journey to the Center of the Earth (Verne) 7, *7*

lava 10, 15
lightning 18
limestone *10*, 11, 22
Lincoln Memorial 22

magma 6–7, *6*, 8, 9, 10, 12, 15, 16–17, 25
magma surges 16–17, *16*
Majal, Mumtaz 23

mantle 6–7, *6*, 8, 9, 10, 16, 25
marble 4, 11, *11*, 13, 21, 22–23, *22*, *23*, 24, *24*, 28
Mauna Loa 15
Meteor Crater 19, *19*
meteorites 18–19
mica 5
Michelangelo 23
migmatite 11
minerals 4, 5, 11, 12, 13, 16, 17, 18–19, 20, 21, 26–27, 29
molecules 7
mountains 4, 9, 14–15, *14*, *15*, 16, 23, 24, 25, 27
Mount Everest 9
Mount Kilimanjaro 15

natural resources 20–21

obsidian 10, *10*
Oregon Caves National Monument 22

Parthenon 22
pet rocks 11
petrologists 5, 27
phyllite 11, 13
plates 8–9, *8*, 11, 14–15, 16, 24, 25, 27
properties 4–5, 13, 26–27

quarries 23, *23*
quartz crystals 5
quartzite 11, 13, 21, 26

rhodochrosite 20, *20*
rifts 8–9
rock hunting 28–29
rocks 4, 6, 10, 24
Rocky Mountains 12, *12*, 14, 25

San Andreas Fault 9
sandstone 11
schist 5, *5*, 11, 13, 20, 26
seafloor spreading 8, *9*
sedimentary rock 4, 10, *10*, 11, 12, 13, 17, 19, 22, 25, *25*, 27
sediments 25
serpentinite 11, 13, 21
shale 11, 16
shock metamorphism 18
Shoemaker, Eugene 19, *19*
slate 11, 13, 20, *21*, 26, 28
soil 6
Split Mountain 17, *17*

Taj Mahal 22, *22*, 23
talc 21
tectonics 8
transform faults 9

Ural Mountains 25

Verne, Jules 7
volcanoes 7, 9, 10, 15, 16

Washington Monument 22
weathering 24, *24*